PLANNING, PERSISTING AND PROSPERING

(Expanded Edition)

PLANNING, PERSISTING AND PROSPERING

(Expanded Edition)

LIBERATE YOURSELF FROM DEBT
BY USING THIS QUICK AND SIMPLE
GUIDE TO UNDERSTANDING
FINANCIAL LITERACY

GARY JOHNSON

**Johnson Enterprises
Oakland, California**

PLANNING, PERSISTING AND PROSPERING

Published by
Johnson Enterprises
Oakland, California
johnsonenterprises777@gmail.com

Gary Johnson, Publisher / Editorial Director
Yvonne Rose/Quality Press. Info, Production Coordinator

Bulk Ordering Information:

Quantity sales. Special discounts are available on quantity purchases by corporations, associations, and others. For details, contact the publisher via email at:
johnsonenterprises777@gmail.com

Copyright © 2020 by Gary Johnson
Paperback ISBN: 978-1-0878-9168-2
Library of Congress Control Number: 2020920823
Made in United States of America

10 9 8 7 6 5 4 3 2 1

CONTENTS

Planning, Persisting and Prospering

INTRODUCTION

"I don't have the money"! Many people have found themselves in this most undesirable disposition, especially when debt collectors attempt to repeatedly contact you by phone, sending intimidating and threatening letters to your home demanding payment. Many of us have been there at some point. Having full control of our debt is essential in order to move towards a more financially independent life.

Living a debt-free lifestyle creates a world of unimaginable opportunities, along with a myriad of serendipitous experiences. However, the journey to becoming completely and unequivocally debt-free, for all intents and purposes, can be an interminable and arduous task.

My total debt in 2012 and 2013 ranged between two and a half million to approximately two and three quarters of a million dollars. ($2,500,000.00-

$2,750,000.00). Through the application of hard work, discipline, self-control and patience, my debt dissipated to forty-five thousand dollars ($45,000.00) within five (5) years. These attributes are exceedingly imperative and can significantly contribute to one's measure of success as it relates to annihilating debt and relegating oneself to a lifestyle of financial freedom. By fostering and cultivating these characteristics, one may simply then adopt the practice of living by a budget, abstaining from compulsive spending, paying on debt as frequently as resources allow and saving 5%-25% of one's income.

Over time, your debt will cease to exist, and your savings will accumulate exponentially, which allows you to posture and position yourself to initiate the regiment of building net worth by making thoughtful and wise investments. Let us explore the effectiveness of hard work, discipline, self-control and patience along with living by a budget, abstaining from compulsive buying, paying down on debt frequently, and building savings and investment accounts in more detail.

SECTION 1

HARD WORK

Many definitions exist describing the concept of "Hard Work". Essentially, hard work is the ability to display a great deal of effort or endurance over a certain time-frame in order to effectively complete a task. Sustaining your capacity to work hard builds confidence and assists in creating an indomitable spirit required to consummate both short term goals and long-term objectives, as it relates to earning income, curing debt and building net worth.

Imagine generating two hundred and fifty thousand to three hundred thousand dollars ($250,000-$300,000) as your annual income. What happens when you lose this income and now you are relegated to earning fifty to one hundred dollars ($50-$100) a day? This was my story.

However, in the face of this monumental challenge of recalibrating to the new normal, working hard each day gave me the hope of eventually elevating myself from this most unimaginable predicament of generating a minuscule level of income and moving towards earning a much higher amount of income.

Eliminating my seemingly insurmountable amount of debt was a motivating factor; and consequently, every day brought hope that my devoted efforts towards working hard would eventually lead to an opportunity of an increased and more viable level of income, thereby allowing me to submit substantially higher payments to my creditors.

Oftentimes, extra shifts, double shifts and side jobs were welcome as it provided the necessary boost required to stay ahead of daily expenses and essentials for living comfortably, along with paying towards my debt. Additionally, working hard at being resourceful was equally imperative, as it created the flow of resources that actually made a prodigious impact on my ability to reduce levels of debt at a more rapid pace.

As I created revenue by liquidating assets and eventually began earning a higher level of income, the ability to pay far above the minimum payment, make frequent payments and settle accounts from fifty cents (.50) to pennies (.01) on the dollar allowed me to completely pay off accounts, thus creating the perfect momentum towards becoming debt free.

Maintaining an accurate accounting of my total debt and the number of accounts remaining was a daily task as it proved to be extremely important as a motivating factor. Also, meticulous accounting allowed me to succinctly set practical and realistic target dates for eliminating any lingering debt.

Therefore, I can say with experience the ability and willingness to work feverishly is the first step to achieving freedom from debt and moving towards financial independence.

DISCIPLINE

Possessing discipline is merely the practice of establishing standards and adhering to a specific pattern of behavior in a consistent manner. Although this is only one of several definitions, incorporating discipline in your everyday life ostensibly requires hard work. My endeavor to eliminate debt could not have been aided without the application of discipline.

The ability to constantly channel the highest percentage of my resources towards paying off debt became the main focal point. Subsequently, focusing on positive actions that would bring me the desired results as it relates to making payments on debt would be at the forefront of my thoughts throughout each day. Positive thoughts play a vital role in achieving any quest.

Waking up every morning with trust, hope and the belief that my hard work and discipline would move me closer to accomplishing the goal of continuing to provide for my family, protect valuable assets still in my possession and extricate myself beyond the financial quagmire, which extenuating circumstances had created in a seemingly short period of time, became an inordinate source of inspiration.

That inspiration sparked the indescribable feelings of being encouraged, enlightened and empowered as my level of discipline began to grow immensely, thereby overshadowing any thoughts of doubt or failure regarding the elimination of my indebtedness. The wonderful feeling of knowing and realizing that discipline would be such an unrelenting and undeterred weapon for conquering debt gave me a drive and passion that was unfathomable along with visions of what possibilities awaited me in the future.

As a result of my "transformation", only a miniscule amount of time would elapse between the moment funds were received into my possession and the time in which these same funds would be utilized for making expenditures to creditors. Wasting time contemplating when to make payments, reasoning why a lower payment amount should be considered or diverting monies to a different cause were all options that became completely foreign.

The action of persistently coagulating a system of "receive and remit" became an integral part of my newly discovered fabric. Over time, my level of discipline became even stronger and began permeating all aspects of my life, which facilitated the establishing of new ideas for a life after debt. Discipline became one of my most "valuable assets" and would prove to be crucial on the road to obliterating the burden of debt.

SELF-CONTROL

Self-control is essentially the ability to manage your actions, feelings and emotions. We as human beings encounter a deluge of temptations every day as products and services are constantly enticing us to partake. Restraint or self-control equips us with the ability to simply abstain from these enticements and avoid the pitfalls and snares of reckless actions particularly associated with buying products and services, along with engaging in various forms of entertainment.

As I began earning more income, the balances in my bank account and the cash I possessed on hand would increase considerably over short intervals of time and these resources gave me a sense of satisfaction and security that had been lost and/or forgotten during the decline into my colossal debt, which still demanded my laser-like attention.

Although the agglomerate of my resources provided me with welcomed buying power and elevated my level of happiness, the overwhelming desire to become debt-free infused me with the much needed prowess for maintaining self-control, and prevented me from excessive spending and making compulsive decisions, which prevented a plentitude of wasted resources.

Envisioning a future free of debt and the feeling derived from that very thought outweighed any imagined pleasures from the misguided actions of needless purchases. The desire to achieve established goals of becoming debt-free and attaining financial independence created and currently upholds my ability to employ self-control.

Additionally, self-control allowed me to begin the practice of making many sacrifices, which assisted in my effort to elude the possibility of experiencing a diversion from my goals. This entailed not dining out with friends for dinner or eating out for lunch with coworkers, bypassing invitations to travel or going on vacations, limiting any activities with my children that demanded expensive fees, and reducing the amount of benevolent acts or contributions to charity.

Desperate times call for desperate measures!!! While challenging at times, these actions became a necessity to remain on course. The combination of hard work, discipline and self-control complemented each other quite well, as this "tremendous trifecta" worked together like a profusely oiled or effectively adjusted machine, thereby producing my desired outcome.

Self-control became ingrained in my "DNA" and gradually created changes in virtually every aspect of my daily life, thus contributing wondrously to the task of curing my debt.

PATIENCE

Patience is the capacity to accept or tolerate delay, trouble or suffering without displaying adverse emotions. Patience is quite possibly the most valuable quality we can exert in difficult circumstances, in comparison to hard work, discipline and self-control. Every aspect of my daily life during my quest to alleviate indebtedness has been greatly enhanced by practicing patience.

Even though I felt confident that my hard work would eventually be rewarded with greater amounts of compensation, I felt impelled to employ patience until better opportunities came to fruition. My ability to exercise discipline did not transpire overnight, for to incorporate discipline into my daily orbit necessitated a vast amount of patience.

Although my level of self-control may have been admirable by some standards, I realistically understood an urgent need to improve the bridling of my actions and reactions to each single event in my life, which was only made possible by utilizing a considerable degree of patience. The ability to wait and anticipate or sit in calm anticipation was conducive to my mental health and allowed me to develop gratitude amidst my precarious predicament. By allowing patience to inundate my thoughts, actions and reactions, the potentiality to mitigate indebtedness became more contemporary.

As I intently watched and closely monitored the dissolution of what was once intimidating debt, which at times was likened to water slowly evaporating from the sidewalk on a balmy summer day, the ability to employ patience reinforced and sustained my desire to remain dedicated and devoted to my primary goal. Also, it gave me the willingness to endure.

The desire to becoming completely debt-free and all the benefits in doing so became valiant and more alive than ever and overshadowed any inclination to moderate or temper my focus; which, in essence, fueled and greatly influenced the metamorphosis and maturation process of executing patience. This enabled me to approach other future life situations with a more composed and long-suffering disposition.

Hard work, discipline and self-control combined with a patience temperament became a formidable force that continued gaining velocity as time progressed. Patience was the bonding agent and adhesive that held everything together, thereby making it possible to achieve the ultimate objective of procuring indebtedness.

SECTION 2

BUDGETING

Creating a budget consists of deriving at an estimate of income and expenditures for a particular timeframe and designating or allocating a certain amount of funds to meet financial obligations and specific areas of need.

Establishing a budget can be easily accomplished by first determining your total income and expenses on a daily, weekly, bi-weekly, monthly, quarterly, semi-annual or annual basis. A budget can fall into three categories: a balanced budget, a budget in which there is a surplus, or a budget resulting in a deficit.

Balanced and surplus budgets offer the comfort of meeting all your financial obligations and having a positive cashflow over a set time-period. Budgets that create a deficit are an indication that total expenses outweigh total income, thereby resulting in a negative cash flow.

Unfortunately, a budget which creates a deficit is exceedingly deleterious as it directly impacts your total debt in a negative fashion. By devising a viable plan for utilizing resources, a sound budget can be an incredible asset as it relates to a steady path to financial independence.

A great starting point would be to list all sources of income received on a regular basis and calculate your total expenses, using the same time period for determining your total income. It's imperative to physically record this information on a notepad or a computer in order to have a clear picture in which you can visualize your financial posture.

By closely examining your income and expenses, adjustments can be made in the form of cost-cutting measures to create a surplus or balanced budget in the case of a budget incurring a deficit. The four previously discussed attributes in section one usher in the necessary tools to reconstruct the contour of your budget and allow the emancipation from a negative cashflow to a balanced budget. However, the real objective is to obviously and eventually produce a positive cashflow which persistently grows over time.

As the schism between income and expenses increases in a positive direction, additional resources required to cure your debt are more readily available and in greater supply to aid and assist you. Also, as mentioned in section one, regarding hard work, working overtime, extra shifts, part-time jobs, along with side or odd jobs and liquidating assets can provide the much-needed resources to create the positive cashflow, thereby paying off your debt and advancing you closer to financial independence.

COMPULSIVE SPENDING

Compulsive spending is buying beyond what is necessary. There is a humongous difference regarding products and services considered to be essential opposed to those that are luxuries or amenities. Determining the distinction between a need or a desire calls for a miniscule amount of cognitive flexibility or common sense. Desires to spend compulsively are and should be completely void of any consideration as we formulate and adhere to our budget.

As we began to widen the gap between income and expenses as a direct result of generating a surplus budget, we must abstain from engaging in compulsive buying, as it can and almost without exception, will completely obliterate your budget and defer the glory of reaching the goal of becoming debt free. In fact, compulsive spending is one of the most detrimental acts a person can commit, as it sends one into a declivity of creating even more debt.

Having fostered and incorporated the ability to administer self-control allows a person to abstain from utilizing valued resources and maintaining the vision of freedom from indebtedness to remain in the forefront of one's psyche. Your self-control provides the much needed strength to resist advertisements for buying a wide array of goods and services, invitations to join friends and family for outings, excursions with that special person and numerous other endeavors, which would all require valuable resources and invested finances that should be channeled towards attaining your desired objective. I realize this may pose an unpleasant challenge, but to forgo all your careful planning and hard work would be antithetic to the primary reason for acquiring financial independence.

Occasionally, an unforeseen expense will arise and shifting monies to a serious or grave matter is acceptable and will indubitably force you to temporarily abandon your budget. However, returning to the regiment of adhering to your budget is key to moving closer to the ultimate prize. Concurrently, it's acceptable to make provisions in your budget for a reasonable amount of entertainment, taking into consideration the limits of how much you can spend and not exceeding that boundary. This will give you some flexibility and fun whilst remaining responsible and staying committed to your goal.

However, it's critical to keep in mind that doing so will delay freedom from debt. Furthermore, it becomes quite rewarding and fulfilling as you decide to shift your entertainment allowance to paying more on a specific account, which will exceed and expedite the timeframe for paying off your debt.

Most notably, exalting and elevating yourself from being a part of the "Consumer Culture" relegates you into the position to succeed. This all may sound stringent or parsimonious, but you must be steadfast. You cannot take one step forward and two steps backwards. Otherwise, you can never move forward at a more appeasing rate. Only after achieving your desired financial goals can you relax your statue and enjoy activities with family and friends.

ELIMINATING DEBT
(DEBT REDUCTION)

Obliterating debt is the practice of paying off balances on revolving credit accounts, installment loans and all other types of financial obligations. Debt in the form of loans can be considered a "necessary evil" in the case of purchasing a home, which in many cases will be the most expensive purchase the average individual will commit to in their lifetime.

Other instances where you may need a loan include purchasing a vehicle, paying for education and accumulating expenses for business endeavors. However, the interest in which you pay renders it seemingly impossible to pay off these types of loans in a reasonable amount of time. Additionally, credit card debt with even higher interest rates only adds to the challenge of annihilating indebtedness.

The most effective way of expediting the process as it pertains to eradicating debt is to pay far above the minimum payment and pay as often as you are paid. This strategy refers to the concept of "receive and remit" mentioned earlier in the discipline section. Also, we can see the vital role that discipline plays in our ability to crush debt in an impressive and incredulous amount of time.

Please note the illustration at the end of this guide of a nearly seven thousand one hundred ($7,100.00) credit card balance that was extinguished in approximately two months. Observe and pay close attention as to the amounts paid and the time intervals in which the payments were submitted. As I paid myself or "received" income earned, I would submit or "remit" a payment to the credit card account, thereby watching the balance rapidly decline.

Along with discipline was the hard work needed to generate the additional income with the sole purpose of extirpating my debt and reaching the main goal of financial independence. An incredible amount of interest can be saved and done so in a noticeably shorter amount of time, particularly in the case of paying off a vehicle or a mortgage.

The difference can come in the form of hundreds of thousands of dollars and shed five, ten or even fifteen years from the original term of the loan. Oftentimes, certain accounts offer early payoff incentives by forgiving hundreds to thousands of dollars from the principal amount of the original loan.

Also, old debts that are lingering on your credit report, which went unpaid and adversely affect your credit score, can be settled for as low as thirty to fifty cents on the dollar. When settling any debt, always attempt to get the lowest settlement amount possible by offering twenty percent (20%) of the balance and hope to settle at fifty percent (50%) or less.

Your ability to eliminate debt will summon all the previously discussed traits working harmoniously in conjunction with each other to accomplish freedom from indebtedness.

SAVING

S aving requires opening an investment or savings account and appropriating funds to the account for the purpose of allowing the funds to remain untouched and accrue interest, thereby allowing your money to work for you and grow.

These funds are not intended to be combined with your finances used to cover daily, essential and necessary expenses, but more so to be reserved for long-term investments or as a safety net. Having now pursued with passion the effective employment of hard work, discipline, self-control, patience along with budgeting, abstaining from compulsive buying and eliminating debt, you have perfectly postured and positioned yourself to launch a "Saving and Investment" campaign that will ensure an expedient trajectory towards financial independence.

Your steadfast self-control working in collusion with discipline will equip you with the restraint to avoid non-discretionary purchases and assiduously channel your resources into investment and savings accounts. Your contributions into these respective accounts should follow the same pattern as paying off debt, when in fact you are now building net worth.

Now it is possible and probable to watch with admirable "patience" as your resources expand exponentially. Income channeled to a form of an investment or savings account with a reasonable interest rate and liquidity options will equip you with the capability to take advantage of a starter or dream home purchase, access to educational opportunities, supplies and equipment for enhancing the profitability of your business, or simply increasing your net worth.

Saving and Investing can be a galvanizing endeavor for you and a source of security and inspiration for family and friends when infused with the same or greater degree of zeal adopted for obliterating indebtedness.

You have now relegated yourself to the position of being the lender and not the borrower. Ironically, your investment accounts will now earn interest generated from loans to the very businesses that you were once indebted to pay interest to regarding your credit accounts.

Most of all, through your saving and investing crusade, you now have the ability and acuteness to assertively and audaciously seek and search better opportunities, which will allow your resources to realize even greater returns.

The time has finally arrived for you to take full control of your finances and enjoy the process of meandering into a life of freedom from meagerly existing in indebtedness to living confidently in a life of "Financial independence"!!!!!!!

SECTION 3

RESTORING/BUILDING CREDIT

C redit restoration is the act of improving your credit score by resolving past due, seriously delinquent and closed accounts due to late payments, non-payments or neglecting to submit payments for an extended period of time, which will appear on your credit report causing your credit score to take a downward turn and create a negative credit history.

Resolving past due and considerably delinquent accounts can be easily accomplished by merely making the minimum payment or past due payment amount in order to bring the account current. Paying off closed accounts as a direct result of non-payment will sometimes necessitate a call to a third party or collection agency to resolve the matter. All three actions will in fact pave the way to restoring and rebuilding your credit.

Occasionally, you may discover an item on your credit report, which you did not initiate.

Consequently, you are not financially responsible for the debt and you can legally dispute the charge as an attempt to have the item removed from your credit report.

As I intimated earlier in the "Eliminating/ Reducing Debt" section, a closed account can generally be settled for thirty cents to fifty cents on the dollar, or even less.

After working diligently for years to establish sound credit, my reasonably good credit score in the low 700's suffered a rapid declension into the low 500's during the financial debacle of 2008. In a quest to reestablish my credit, these were the several steps required to begin and complete the process:

Step 1 - Acquire a copy of my credit report

Step 2 - Identify each legitimate open and closed account(s)

Step 3 - Contact the creditor(s) and settle/pay off the account(s)

(ALWAYS accurately record the name of the person assisting you, date, time and amount agreed upon as the payoff/settlement offer.

(ALWAYS ask for the payoff/settlement letter in writing or an email for your records)

(The settlement letter/email should contain the words "Paid in Full")

Step 4 - Contact the credit reporting agency, inform them of the payoff/settlement and asked to have the negative account removed from your credit report. (Transunion, Equifax, Experian)

(Before or after receiving the settlement letter/email)

Step 5 - The settlement letter/email should be attached to your credit report upon receipt.

(Consider placing a copy of your bank/credit card statement used to settle the account)

(Indicate on your credit report the account has been "Paid in Full", along with the date)

Meticulously maintaining your records can help you to elude the possibility of paying off an account twice and can prove to be helpful when applying for new credit accounts or loans. Almost invariably, closed credit card accounts can be reopened in time, thereby allowing you to rebuild your credit and thus increase your overall credit score. Also, secured credit cards and line of credit accounts will aid you in building your credit worthiness.

As you consistently make on time payments thus strengthening your credit history (35%), maintain low balances/usage on your active credit accounts (30%), retain the oldest accounts for the purpose of long standing credit (15%) , abstain from accumulating too many inquiries in a 24 month period, which should be no more than 6 (10%) and open a healthy mix of both revolving credit accounts (credit cards/lines of credit) and installment credit accounts (car loans/set payments and time period 10%).

These are the 5 factors that influence your credit score the most, which is also the application employed to build a good or excellent credit score. By utilizing these 5 factors to my benefit, my credit score was restored to the mid 700's, which could transpire expeditiously based on your level of motivation.

Although you may experience an occasional fluctuation in your credit score, over time the positive impact on your credit score will become quite noticeable and lead to great results.

INVESTING IN
REAL ESTATE

Essentially, real estate is property consisting of land, land accompanied with a building and land along with natural resources such as crops or water and minerals.

Residential real estate, which is the focus of this guide, usually consists of a single-family residence or a multi-family structure dwelling available for occupancy. Although residential real estate is generally for non-business purposes, it can be utilized to conduct certain types of business activities.

Flats, which is usually an individual unit in a multi-unit building, condominiums, townhouses and other dwellings are all considered to be in the major category of residential real estate, as well.

My first property was a two-bedroom, one bath condominium on the South Hill in Spokane, Washington, which was over thirty years ago in the month of August prior to the Gulf War in 1990. My first buying experience left me with the indelible impression that purchasing real estate is by far one of the most forgiving investments one can engage or endeavor to invest in as a wealth-building vehicle.

Although a property may depreciate at some point, over time and/or eventually it will appreciate, oftentimes exceeding its original value. The benefits of investing in real estate include, but are not limited to creating passive income, stable cash flow in the form of rental income, profit through various business activities, tax advantages, diversification and leverage.

Making the decision to purchase a residential property as your primary residence or any type of real estate as an investment can be one of the most exciting and exuberating commitments in one's lifetime.

By applying everything learned in the previous sections of this guide, you are endowed with the acuteness and in the perfect locale for launching an efficacious plan to assure success. The first step is to visit a lending institution for the purpose of educating and familiarizing yourself with the loan process.

Lending institutions such as banks, credit unions, finance companies and individual brokers will have requirements that must be met to initiate the process regarding the production of some critical documentation.

Although you are at liberty to begin looking at homes, its best to contact a lender and attain pre-approval status to avoid looking at homes that may be beyond your price range. Pre-qualifying is basically an estimate of how much you can afford to spend on a home and therefore less valuable than a pre-approval.

The pre-approval process determines the amount of the loan a financial institution is willing to actually extend to you for the real estate purchase. It's during the pre-approval process when the lender verifies your employment, income, assets, credit score and the pertinent documentation.

Meticulously maintaining your records provides you with easy access to bank statements, tax returns and statement of earnings within minutes and allows you to move more expeditiously through the first stage of the pre-approval process.

Once the process has been completed, the lender will provide you with a pre-approval letter; and subsequently, equips you with a stronger negotiating position with potential sellers. Also, this is the time in which your lender will discuss with you the various loan options and mortgage products. Fixed and adjustable rate mortgages, government sponsored VA, FHA, USDA and jumbo loans, non-qualifying and customizable loans are just a few options available, which can all be tailored to fit your specific need or desire.

First time home buyer programs, which allow you to take advantage of zero down payment or low percentage down payment opportunities, can make the buying experience much easier and well within reach for lower income families. It's now time to find a great bargain or that "DREAM HOME"!!!

Additionally, there are other ways in which to purchase residential real estate or investment property, such as tax lien sales, pre-foreclosures, foreclosed/REO's (Real Estate Owned by the Bank) and estate sales. Each of these real estate transactions has a unique set of rules and entails some research to familiarize yourself with the procedures for completing the sales transaction specific to the purchase.

Most importantly, a multitude of family members can enjoy the benefits derived from owning real estate as it creates generational wealth and is therefore bequeathed to many generations.

CONCLUSION

Acquiring the ultimate prize calls for great sacrifice. Initially, I mentioned the staggering amount of debt unmasked of approximately two and three quarters of a million dollars (2,750,000.00). This debt was in the form of real estate investments, which consisted of a family home, my primary residence and two rental properties.

Reverting back to my statement about making great sacrifices, all real estate investments had to eventually be liquidated, thereby expelling the mortgages on each property. Along with the mortgages was a cosmic IRS tax bill, which stemmed mainly through short sale transactions and ranged in the hundreds of thousands. The bill was settled for pennies on the dollar through an "offer in compromise".

Expeditiously extinguishing the remaining amount of debt will continue to be the omphalos of 2020. I refuse to let my massive debt define me as I continue to strive to be an entirely different vein. The ability to becoming debt-free, or any goal, begins with a thought. It is that very thought coupled with the desire to achieve a specific objective that guides and navigates your every action.

Aside from some obvious circumstances and preconditions, everyone is endowed with the ability to achieve success. Success is a subjective term; and consequently, everyone's portrait of success may vary from person to person. However, everything needed to becoming successful is within our souls and it is therefore a matter of extrapolating that which is within, along with commissioning anything and everything that is extraneous of one's self to serve as a resource, thus benefiting our cause.

Acquiring something new will require relinquishing something antiquated. The antediluvian thoughts, behavior and actions that once created debt must be transformed into advanced concepts, attitudes and efforts that generates wealth.

"Hard Work", "Discipline", "Self-Control" and "Patience" are just a few enormously crucial qualities that will bring forth much good fortune in all aspects of your life. Therefore, one must endeavor to covet these exceedingly imperative attributes by any reasonable means necessary and begin the process of becoming free of indebtedness and accomplishing financial independence.

Financial Independence can range from thousands to millions of dollars and beyond in net worth. Creativity in generating resources will be a welcomed ally and aid you well on your path to becoming debt-free. By integrating all of these steps described in this guide into your action plan for success, you are competently fulfilling the mantra that is the title of this work.

When you plan for your goals and remain persistent in your actions, it will most certainly lead you to prosper. Achieving any objective can be a daunting task; but approach it with a positive and hopeful attitude and you're halfway there!

Above all things, "NEVER LOSE YOUR FAITH"!!!!!!!

STATEMENT #1

BALANCE SUMMARY

Previous Balance	$7,057.12
- Payments	$558.00
- Other Credits	$0.00
+ Cash Advances	$0.00
+ Purchases, Balance Transfers & Other Charges	$0.00
+ Fees Charged	$0.00
+ Interest Charged	$60.97
= New Balance	$6,560.09

Payment Information	
New Balance	$6,560.09
Minimum Payment	$127.00
Payment Due Date	09/01/2019

Transactions

Payments

	07/13	Online Payment	$58.00
	07/21	Online Payment	$500.00

TOTAL PAYMENTS FOR THIS PERIOD	$558.00

TOTAL FEES FOR THIS PERIOD	$0.00

STATEMENT #2

BALANCE SUMMARY

Previous Balance	$6,560.09
- Payments	$2,560.09
- Other Credits	$0.00
+ Cash Advances	$0.00
+ Purchases, Balance Transfers & Other Charges	$0.00
+ Fees Charged	$0.00
+ Interest Charged	$21.81
= New Balance	$4,021.81

Payment Information
New Balance	$4,021.81
Minimum Payment	$63.00
Payment Due Date	10/01/2019

Transactions

Payments
08/12	Online Payment		$560.10
08/19	Online Payment		$1,500.00
08/26	Online Payment		$499.99

TOTAL PAYMENTS FOR THIS PERIOD	$2,560.09

TOTAL FEES FOR THIS PERIOD	$0.00

STATEMENT #3

BALANCE SUMMARY

Previous Balance	$4,021.81
− Payments	$4,021.81
− Other Credits	$0.00
+ Cash Advances	$0.00
+ Purchases, Balance Transfers & Other Charges	$0.00
+ Fees Charged	$0.00
+ Interest Charged	$0.00
= New Balance	$0.00

Payment Information
   New Balance $4,021.81
   Minimum Payment $63.00
   Payment Due Date   11/01/2019

Transactions

Payments

09/10	Online Payment		$521.81
09/13	Online Payment		$500.00
09/16	Online Payment		$500.00
09/19	Online Payment		$500.00
09/23	Online Payment		$1,000.00
09/25	Online Payment		$500.00
09/26	Online Payment		$250.00
09/27	Online Payment		$250.00

TOTAL PAYMENTS FOR THIS PERIOD $4,021.81

TOTAL FEES FOR THIS PERIOD $0.00

DEBT-FREE NOTES

_____

_____

_____

_____

_____

_____

_____

_____

_____

_____

_____

_____

_____

_____

_____

_____

_____

_____

_____

_____

_____

_____

_____

_____

_____

_____

_____

_____

_____

_____

_____

_____

_____

_____

_____

_____

_____

_____

_____

_____

_____

_____

_____

_____

_____

_____

_____

_____

ABOUT THE AUTHOR

Gary Johnson is a native of San Francisco, California. Growing up, he developed an affinity for numbers, and studied business administration in college whilst beginning a career in banking and finance.

Prior to the completion of college, Johnson taught English for a year in a foreign country, which inspired him to find his true calling - helping and educating others, especially in matters of finance. While initiating a campaign of real estate investing in several states, he realized his passion for teaching and the desire to help others achieve the "American Dream." This has brought him a considerable degree of fulfillment

Through extensive knowledge and experience, Johnson advises and emphasizes for clients to build strong credit, regulate indebtedness, and accumulate resources in order to help pave the way to financial independence. It is his hope that these tangible methods can be of help to others like they were for him.

Johnson attributes much of his success to his mother, father, and seven siblings, whom he says have supported him greatly in his endeavors and encouraged him to lead a life of serving others.

Planning, Persisting and Prospering: Liberate Yourself From Debt by Using This Quick and Simple Guide to Understanding Financial Literacy is Gary Johnson's first published book. For further information, visit: www.garykjohnson.com

CPSIA information can be obtained
at www.ICGtesting.com
Printed in the USA
BVHW090455070521
606654BV00008B/1702